D1709529

LET'S EAT!

Mealtime Around the World

by
LYNNE MARIE

illustrated by
PARWINDER SINGH

beaming books
MINNEAPOLIS

Copyright © 2019 Beaming Books

Published in 2019 by Beaming Books, an imprint of 1517 Media. All rights reserved. No part of this book may be reproduced without the written permission of the publisher. Email copyright@1517.media. Printed in the United States of America.

25 24 23 22 21 20 19   1 2 3 4 5 6 7 8 9

ISBN: 9781506451947

Written by Lynne Marie

Illustrated by Parwinder Singh

Library of Congress Cataloging-in-Publication Data

Names: Lynne Marie, author. | Singh, Pawinder, illustrator.
Title: Let's eat! : meal time around the world / written by Lynne Marie ;
    illustrated by Pawinder Singh.
Description: Minneapolis, MN : Beaming Books, 2019. | Audience: Age 4-8.
Identifiers: LCCN 2019004271 | ISBN 9781506451947 (hardcover : alk. paper)
Subjects: LCSH: Food--Juvenile literature. | International cooking--Juvenile
    literature. | Food habits--Juvenile literature.
Classification: LCC TX355 .L97 2019 | DDC 641.59--dc23
LC record available at https://lccn.loc.gov/2019004271

VN0004589;9781506451947;SEPT2019

Beaming Books

510 Marquette Avenue
Minneapolis, MN 55402
Beamingbooks.com

From sunup to sundown, people all over the world plan
their day around the same thing: food! Food of every kind—
whether salty or sweet, soft or crunchy, plain or mixed,
eaten at different times or in different manners—
can be found during mealtimes around the world.

Congee is a comfort food in China. It is the first food besides milk that babies eat. It is also given to people when they are feeling ill, especially with a stomachache.

In China, Yu Yan eats a rice porridge for breakfast called congee. Sometimes squid caught by her father is mixed in. She slurps loudly to show how much she likes it.

But hurry, Yu Yan, school starts soon!

What do you put in your porridge?

Since 1200 BCE, Chinese people have used chopsticks for cooking and eating utensils instead of forks and knives. Spoons are still used for soup.

In Iceland, Pétur enjoys a bowl of thick yogurt-like cheese called skyr topped with red currant jam. Sometimes he sprinkles granola and nuts or stone fruits on his skyr. Yum!

Let's go, Pétur! The fish are biting!

What is your favorite fish to eat?

During the shortest winter days in Iceland, daylight lasts only about three hours. From May until July, daylight can last up to twenty-four hours!

Brown trout swim in Iceland's rivers and lakes and are the main ingredient in many classic Icelandic dishes.

In Peru's mountain highlands, Luz wakes early to tend to her grandfather's llamas. First she eats a hot, creamy soup made of pureed, freeze-dried potatoes called chuño cola. Breakfast is usually leftovers from last night's meal.

Come, llamas! Now it's your turn to eat!

What would your breakfast include if you were eating last night's leftovers?

Llamas are members of the camel family. They can grow up to six feet tall. People in the Andes Mountains use llamas to carry heavy loads. They use llamas' fleece for fabrics to make clothing, blankets, and rugs.

Potatoes are a staple of the Peruvian diet. The people of Peru started growing potatoes about 10,000 years ago and grow a variety of colors: red, blue, purple, yellow, pink, and white.

In the Philippines, Rosamie helps her family by filling plates with spamsilog—fried SPAM, eggs, and garlic rice that she made herself. Sometimes, her family eats tapsilog, dried beef and rice, or hotsilog, hot dogs and rice.

Rosamie cleans her plate. *More spamsilog, please!*

How do you help with mealtime in your family?

SPAM, spiced ham in a can, first came to the Philippines during World War II. US soldiers used SPAM because it didn't need to be cooked or refrigerated.

On the Caribbean island of Jamaica, Zhade spoons spicy ground beef onto thin discs of pastry dough. She works with her mother to pinch the edges together. Once baked and cooled, the flaky bread packets are delicious on their own or stuffed into coco bread to make sandwiches.

Call your siblings, Zhade—time to eat!

What kind of savory pastries do you like to eat?

Coco bread is a soft, sweet bread. When wrapped around and cooked with a beef patty, coco bread takes on some of the spice from the beef.

At Christmastime, Jamaican children enjoy Jamaican Fruit Cake, a traditional cake for the holiday.

In France, Camille eats a big lunch at school. In the cantine, she enjoys a healthy, four-course meal with her friends. First comes a cucumber and tomato salad, then a main course of roast beef with cooked broccoli. Next, a small plate of cheese, finished with apple tart for dessert.

Lunch is over, Camille! Back to class!

What do you eat for your school lunch?

There's no school for French children on Wednesday afternoons. Instead, many attend on Saturday mornings.

France is well-known for its food, including baguettes, chocolate mousse, crepes, French Onion Soup, and King's Cake.

In the highlands of Scotland, Logan comes home from school to find his Auntie Margaret busy with baking day. She serves him a snack of scones and clotted cream, with a cup of tea.

It's getting dark, Logan! Time to call the cows home!

Which baked goods does your family make together?

Some children slather their scones with tangy Marmalade made from oranges.

The Highland Cow is a hearty type of cattle bred to survive cold winters in the Scottish Highlands. They have long horns and wavy, wooly coats and can produce milk for a small family.

In Madagascar, Sitraka snacks on crispy Kaka Pizon to give him energy while studying. This potato chip-like snack is sometimes spiced with chili paste.

Sitraka enjoys the hot spice on his tongue. He takes a long drink of water and eats another.

Which spicy foods have you tried?

Kaka pizon literally means "pigeon poop." But don't worry, it's doesn't taste like it!

Dishes in Madagascar aren't typically spicy, but a chili paste called sakay can be added to any meal. Be careful with sakay; it's incredibly hot!

In India, Priya enjoys Tandoori chicken at her favorite restaurant.

After returning home, Priya watches a cricket match on television with her family.

What is your favorite sport to watch?

Tandoori chicken is marinated in yogurt and spices then roasted in a tandoor, a round clay oven.

Cricket is the most popular sport in India. It is played on a field with two teams of eleven players, who use a ball and a flat bat to score points.

Lingonberry jam is a sweet condiment that doesn't just go on pancakes. It is often added to many different dishes: porridge, black pudding, and even meatballs.

Like many Swedish people, Hugo's family practices a tradition from the fifteenth century: on Thursdays, he eats pea soup and pancakes with lingonberry jam. Perfect for keeping warm on a cold winter night.

Don't eat all of the jam, Hugo!

What do you like to put on pancakes?

In the era of the Vikings, people preserved their meat by salting and drying it. Even with fridges and freezers, Swedes continue to dry and salt meat, giving it a unique flavor.

In the United States, Janie spins on a stool at her uncle's restaurant. She watches eagerly as he ladles a thick seafood gumbo into containers for her to take home for dinner.

Be careful, Janie. Don't drop dinner!

What's your favorite restaurant meal?

Gumbo is a West African term for the vegetable okra. Okra has a mild flavor and is often used to thicken gumbo, especially seafood gumbos.

There is no one way to make gumbo. Gumbo can be made with chicken, sausage, seafood, or vegetables. Most gumbos are served with rice.

It's time for dessert in Egypt! Mandisa shares basbousa with her family. A syrup of rose- or orange-blossom water poured on the coconut cake makes it extra sweet. Mandisa loves treats!

Mandisa shares a piece with her brother. He loves the slightly crunchy top, while she likes the airy center best.

How do you share your favorite foods?

In Egypt, left hands are considered unclean. So only right hands are used to touch food and pass dishes.

Many favorite foods in Egypt, including figs, dates, green vegetables, and onions, have been eaten there since the ancient times.

Nigeria is a tropical climate where lots of different fruits grow. The most common fruits are oranges, melons, grapefruits, mangoes, bananas, and pineapple.

In Nigeria, Chetachi helps make a sweet dessert salad with the ripe fruits purchased at the market today. He mixes mangoes, papayas, pineapples, and apples in a bowl, then tops them with sweetened, flaked coconut.

Make sure to share your dessert with your sister, Chetachi!

What fruits grow where you live?

Food is an important part of Nigerian hospitality. It is considered rude if you don't share a meal when you have a visitor.

With over 7.5 billion people on the planet, it's no wonder there are so many different foods that people enjoy eating. Food brings people together, creates community, and helps us grow healthy and strong.

What new meal do you want to try?

ABOUT THE AUTHOR

Lynne Marie is the author of several children's books, including *The Star in the Christmas Play*, illustrated by Lorna Hussey. Her stories, poems, and folk tales have appeared in many magazines, and she is an on-staff writer for Jon and Laura Bard's Children's Book Insider and a book reviewer. When she's not traveling around the world or planning vacations for clients as a travel agent, she lives on a lake in South Florida with her daughter Kayla Michelle, son Kevin, a Schipperke named Anakin, and several resident water birds.

ABOUT THE ILLUSTRATOR

Parwinder Singh was born and lives in the "Steel City" Jamshedpur, India—among diverse cultures, where people love to celebrate their traditional festivals. Singh has always loved to draw and color, and now his childhood hobby has become his profession. Working as an illustrator has given him the opportunity to explore more art styles and travel to different places.